This book is dedicated to my beautiful daughters Gabriella & Sofia, may you both continue to grow as beautifully as you've been thus far, realizing always the power you have to choose not only your thoughts and feelings but your decisions & actions too.

To my mindfulness teacher Randy Knipping, for passionately passing down timeless lessons that have been a gift in my life

To my wife, thank you for believing in me always

One Friday afternoon at school, Rachel's teacher Mr. Williams walked up to her and gave her a gift.
"I know it's your birthday tomorrow, this gift is from the teachers," he said.

"Oh wow!" exclaimed Rachel, "Thank you so much Mr. Williams! Can I open it now?" she asked.

"Maybe you can open it later, at home with your family!" Mr. Williams suggested.

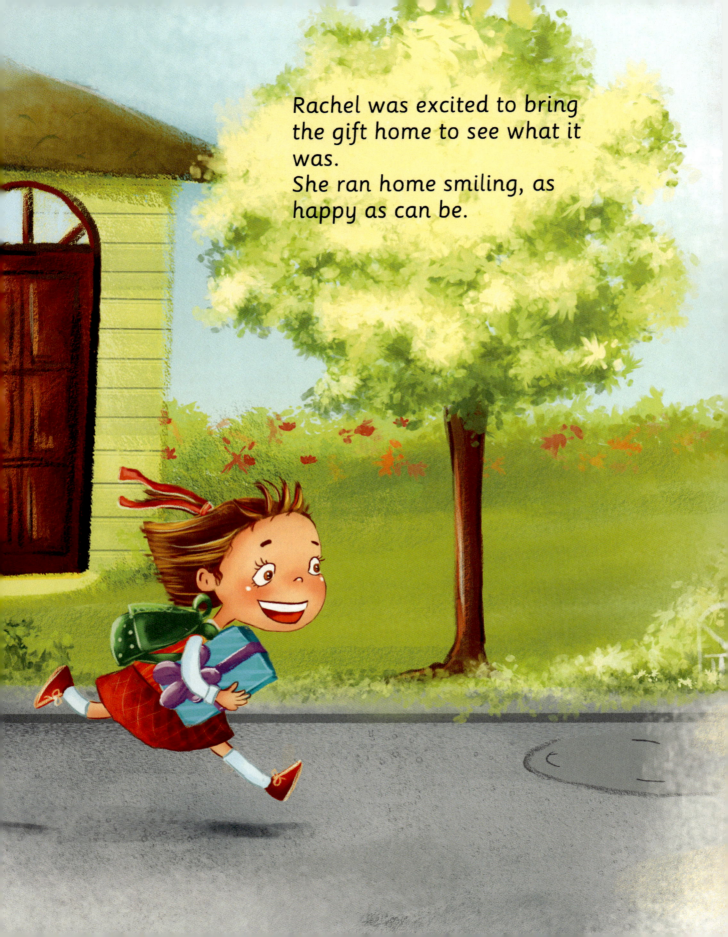

Rachel was excited to bring the gift home to see what it was.
She ran home smiling, as happy as can be.

Once home, Rachel saw some friends playing near by. She dropped her school bag at the front door and headed straight to the neighbourhood park to play hide and seek.

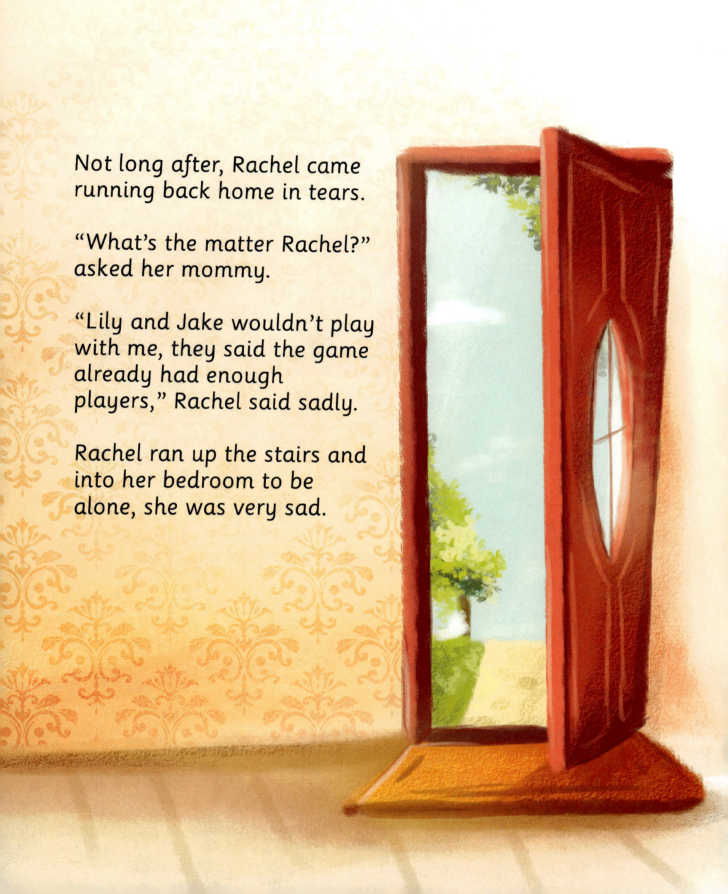

Not long after, Rachel came running back home in tears.

"What's the matter Rachel?" asked her mommy.

"Lily and Jake wouldn't play with me, they said the game already had enough players," Rachel said sadly.

Rachel ran up the stairs and into her bedroom to be alone, she was very sad.

After a few minutes, Rachel settled down, she wiped her tears and noticed the gift her teacher gave her earlier that day.
She reached over and opened the gift.

When Rachel opened up the gift, she saw that it was a book called
"The Rollercoaster." She was very interested and started to look through the pages, wondering what she could learn about one of her favourite amusement park attractions.

Rachel read through the book and didn't stop until she finished it.

She loved learning about all the different rides… but most of all she learned something new!

Rachel learned that our thoughts and feelings can sometimes take us on a rollercoaster ride.

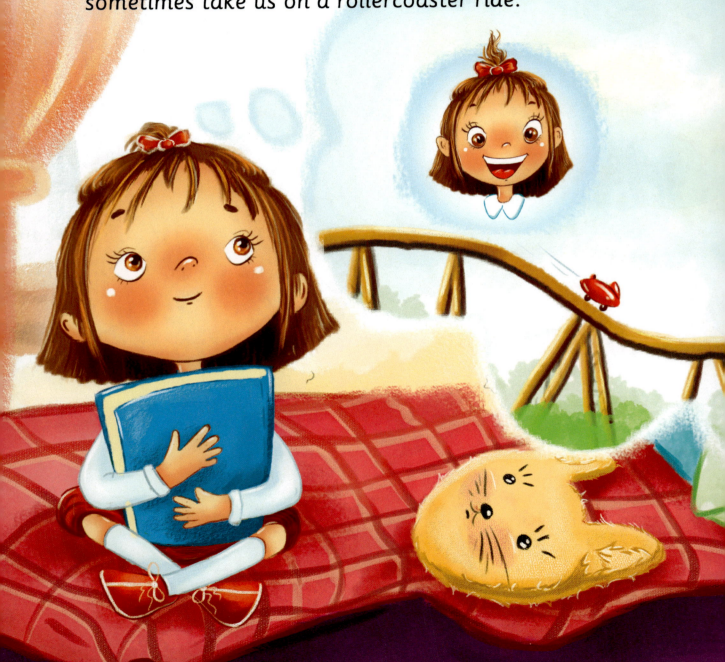

She learned that thoughts and feelings come and go, and they can even go up or down or be fun or sad.

Some rides are really fun, like playing games with her friends!

Some rides can seem really scary, like going into a dark room all alone.

Then suddenly Rachel had a thought!

"Maybe I can choose to go on rides I like, and choose not go on the ones I don't like."

"Maybe I can just watch my thoughts and observe my feelings, even if I don't want to go on the ride," she said happily.

As Rachel read through the book, she discovered a very special secret.

She learned that a great way she can start to choose which thoughts to ride, she would need to practice taking a deep and slow breath as soon as she started to feel angry, sad or scared.

Before getting scared or upset, sad or angry, she would need to take one slow, deep breath, and remember that she now has the power to choose.

"Do I really need to feel sad right now? Or, can I just watch this feeling pass?" she asked herself.

Suddenly, Rachel felt more in control of her feelings!

She has the power to choose whether to go on the rollercoaster, or just watch it go by.

The next day at school, Rachel was playing hopscotch during recess with her friend Lily.

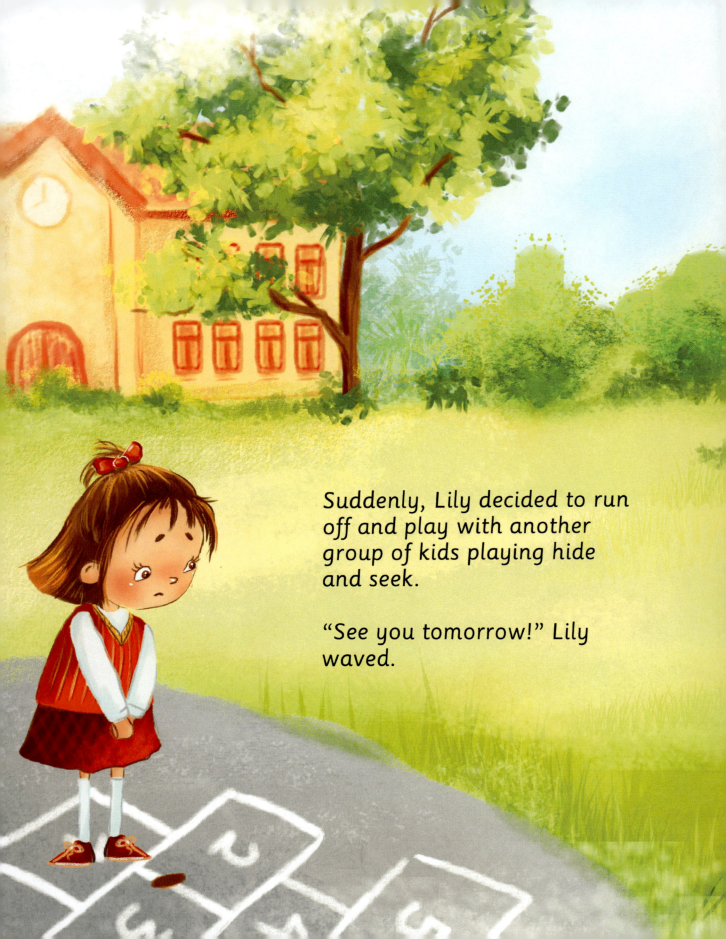

Suddenly, Lily decided to run off and play with another group of kids playing hide and seek.

"See you tomorrow!" Lily waved.

Rachel felt sadness arise in her heart. As she started to feel upset and just before she was going to cry, she remembered the book about the rollercoasters!

She took a deep, slow breath and watched the sadness rollercoaster go up and zoom away.

Rachel felt strong and proud that she was able to see the sadness but not stay on the ride.

Suddenly, Rachel heard a call. "Rachel…. Hey Rachel… can you play with us?" said the group of kids playing hide and seek.

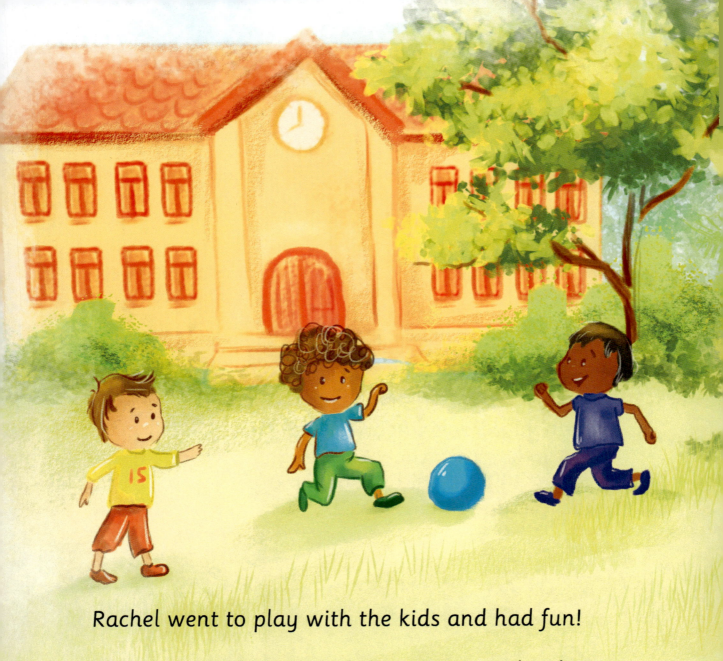

Rachel went to play with the kids and had fun!

That day, Rachel learned that it's normal to have moments of sadness or fear but now she has the power to choose whether or not she wants to stay feeling a certain way, watch a feeling go by or choose a different response.

Manufactured by Amazon.ca
Bolton, ON

39694171R00021